To Parents and Teachers:

We hope you and the children will enjoy reading this story in English and French. The story is simply told, but not *simplfied,* so the language of the French and the English is quite natural but there is a lot of repetition.

At the back of the book is a small picture dictionary with the key words and how to pronounce them. There is also a simple pronunciation guide to the whole story on the last page.

Here are a few suggestions for using the book:

• Read the story aloud in English first, to get to know it. Treat it like any other picture book: look at the pictures, talk about the story and the characters and so on.

• Then look at the picture dictionary and say the French names for the key words. Ask the children to repeat them. Concentrate on speaking the words out loud, rather than reading them.

• Go back and read the story again, this time in English and French. Don't worry if your pronunciation isn't quite correct. Just have fun trying it out. Check the guide at the back of the book, if necessary, but you'll soon pick up how to say the French words.

• When you think you and the children are ready, you can try reading the story in French only. Ask the children to say it with you. Only ask them to read it if they are eager to try. The spelling could be confusing and discourage them.

• Above all, encourage the children and give them lots of praise. Little children are usually quite unselfconscious and this is excellent for building up confidence in a foreign language.

First paperback edition for the United States, its Dependencies, Canada, and the Philippines published 1998 by Barron's Educational Series, Inc. Text © Copyright 1998 by b small publishing, Surrey, England.

Address all inquiries to: Barron's Educational Series, Inc., 250 Wireless Boulevard, Hauppauge, New York 11788 • http//www.barronseduc.com
International Standard Book Number 0-7641-5126-6   Library of Congress Catalog Card Number 98-72552
Printed in Hong Kong   9 8 7 6 5 4 3 2 1

What's for supper?

Qu'est-ce qu'on mange ce soir?

Mary Risk
Pictures by Carol Thompson
French by Christophe Dillinger

BARRON'S

We're making supper tonight, Mom.

C'est *nous* qui allons préparer le dîner ce soir, maman.

It's going to be a surprise.

Ça va être une surprise.

Do we need cheese?

Il nous faut du fromage?

Yes, we need cheese, and ham too.

Oui, il nous faut du fromage et
aussi du jambon.

Do we need flour?

Il nous faut de la farine?

Yes.

Oui.

What about potatoes?
Do we need them?

Et des pommes de terre?
Il nous en faut?

No, we don't need potatoes.

Non, on n'a pas besoin de pommes
de terre.

But we need tomatoes
and mushrooms.

Mais il nous faut des tomates et
des champignons.

Let's put some olives in it!

Mettons-y des olives!

Oh no! I don't like olives.

Ah non! Je n'aime pas les olives.

How much is all that?

C'est combien tout ça?

What are you going to make?
Please tell me. Please!

No! It's a surprise!

Qu'est-ce que vous allez préparer?
Allez, dites-moi, s'il vous plaît!

Non! C'est une surprise!

Here we are home again.

Nous voilà rentrés à la maison.

Don't come into the kitchen, Mom.
Please!

N'entre pas dans la cuisine, maman.
S'il te plaît!

Supper's ready. It's...

Le dîner est prêt. C'est...

a pizza!

une pizza!

Pronouncing French

Don't worry if your pronunciation isn't quite correct. The important thing is to be willing to try. The pronunciation guide here will help but it cannot be completely accurate:

- Read the guide as naturally as possible, as if it were English.
- Put stress on the letters in *italics,* e.g., from*aj*.
- Don't roll the r at the end of the word, for example, in the French word **le** (the): ler.

If you can, ask a French person to help and move on as soon as possible to speaking the words without the guide.

Note: French adjectives usually have two forms, one for masculine and one for feminine nouns. They often look very similar but are pronounced slightly differently, e.g., **prêt** and **prête** (see next page).

Words Les Mots

leh moh

to cook supper
préparer le dîner

prehpah-*reh* ler deen*eh*

tonight
ce soir
ser swah

surprise
la surprise
la s-yoor*preez*

cheese
le fromage
ler from*aj*

ham
le jambon
ler shom*boh*

flour
la farine
lah far-*een*

tomato
la tomate
lah tom*at*

potato
la pomme de terre
lah pom der *tair*

olive
l'olive
lol*eev*

mushroom
le champignon
ler shom-peen-*yoh*

pizza
la pizza
lah peet*zah*

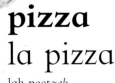

ready
prêt/prête
preh/pret

home/house

la maison

lah may*zoh*

Mom

maman

ma-*moh*

Dad

papa

pa-*pah*

kitchen

la cuisine

la kwee*zeen*

yes

oui

wee

no

non

noh

please

s'il te plaît/
s'il vous plaît

seel ter pleh/seel voo pleh

A simple guide to pronouncing this French story

Qu'est-ce qu'on mange ce soir?
*kesk*oh monsh ser swah

C'est *nous* qui allons préparer
seh *noo* kee al-*oh* prehpah-*reh*

le dîner ce soir, maman.
ler deen*eh* ser swah, ma-*moh*

Ça va être une surprise.
sah vah *etr'* yoon s-yoor*preez*

Il nous faut du fromage?
eel noo fo dew from*aj*

Oui, il nous faut du fromage
wee, eel noo fo dew from*aj*

et aussi du jambon.
eh oh*see* dew shom*boh*

Il nous faut de la farine?
eel noo fo der lah far-*een*

Oui.
wee

Et des pommes de terre?
eh deh pom der *tair*

Il nous en faut?
eel noo*zoh* fo

**Non, on n'a pas besoin de
pommes de terre.**
noh, oh nah pah b'zwah der pom
der *tair*

Mais il nous faut des tomates
meh eel noo fo deh tom*at*

et des champignons.
eh deh shom-peen-*yoh*

Mettons-y des olives!
met-o*zee* dezo*leev*

**Ah non! Je n'aime pas les
olives.**
ah noh, sh' nem pah lezo*leev*

C'est combien tout ça?
seh kombee-*yah* too sah

**Qu'est-ce que vous allez
préparer?**
kesker voozal-*eh* prehpah-*reh*

Allez, dites-moi, s'il vous plaît!
al-*eh*, deet mwah seel voo pleh

Non! C'est une surprise!
noh, set yoon s-yoor*preez*

Nous voilà rentrés à la maison.
noo vwah-*lah* ront*reh* ah lah
may*zoh*

**N'entre pas dans la cuisine,
maman. S'il te plaît!**
nontr' pah doh lah kwee*zeen*,
ma-*moh*. seel ter pleh

Le dîner est prêt. C'est...
ler deen*eh* eh preh, seh

une pizza!
yoon peet*sah*

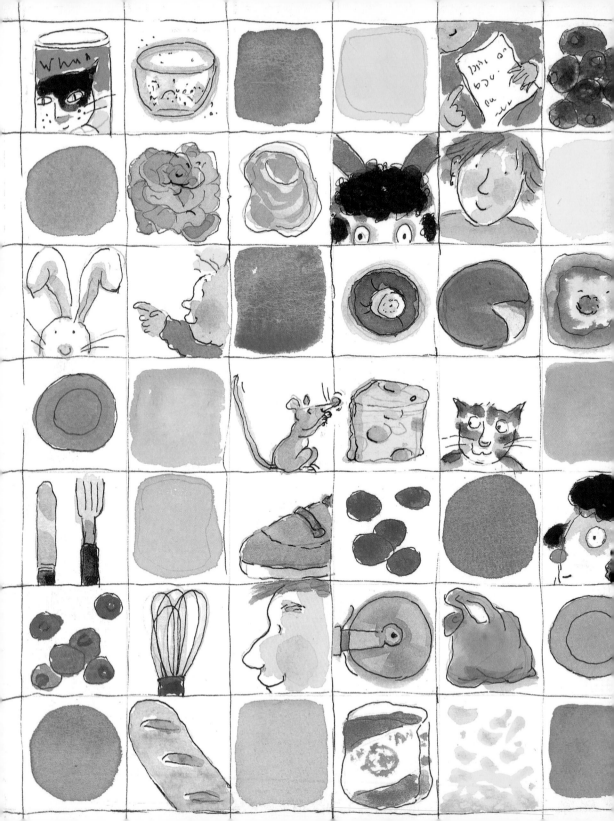